CONTENTS

FREEDOM IS IN PERIL

DEFEND IT WITH ALL YOUR MIGHT

HOME FRONT POSTERS
OF THE
SECOND WORLD WAR

Susannah Walker

SHIRE PUBLICATIONS

Published in Great Britain in 2012 by Shire Publications Ltd,
Midland House, West Way, Botley, Oxford OX2 0PH,
United Kingdom.
44-02 23rd Street, Suite 219, Long Island City, NY 11101,
USA.

E-mail: shire@shirebooks.co.uk   www.shirebooks.co.uk

© 2012 Susannah Walker.

A CIP catalogue record for this book is available from the
British Library.

Shire Library no. 682.   ISBN-13: 978 0 74781 142 8

Susannah Walker has asserted her right under the
Copyright, Designs and Patents Act, 1988, to be identified
as the author of this book.

Designed by Myriam Bell Design, UK and typeset in
Perpetua and Gill Sans.

Printed in China through Worldprint Ltd.

12 13 14 15 16   10 9 8 7 6 5 4 3 2 1

COVER IMAGE
Detail from the poster on page 20.

TITLE PAGE IMAGE
Salvage of every kind was a popular subject for posters,
and hundreds were produced.

CONTENTS PAGE IMAGE
The GPO was one of many organisations that advertised
the need to use its services less rather than more.

ACKNOWLEDGEMENTS
I would like to thank the people and institutions who have
allowed me to use illustrations, which are acknowledged as
follows:

Barter Books, page 46 (top); Debenhams, page 46
(bottom); Design Council/University of Brighton Design
Archives, page 43; Imperial War Museum, pages 4, 6 (top
right), 7, 8, 9, 11, 15 (bottom), 18, 23, 25 (both), 28
(top), 29 (top right), 30, 34, 37, 38 (both), 39: Royal
Society for the Prevention of Accidents, page 30; Swann
Galleries, pages 14 (right), and 16; Woolley & Wallis
Auctioneers, pages 22 and 24.

I would also like to acknowledge the unpublished PhD
thesis *The Planning, Design and Reception of British Home Front
Posters of the Second World War*, by Dr Bex Lewis.

IMPERIAL WAR MUSEUM COLLECTIONS
Some of the photos in this book come from the Imperial
War Museum's huge collections which cover all aspects of
conflict involving Britain and the Commonwealth since the
start of the twentieth century. These rich resources are
available online to search, browse and buy at
www.iwmcollections.org.uk. In addition to Collections
Online, you can visit the Visitor Rooms where you can
explore over 8 million photographs, thousands of hours of
moving images, the largest sound archive of its kind in the
world, thousands of diaries and letters written by people
in wartime, and a huge reference library. To make an
appointment, call (020) 7416 5320, or e-mail
mail@iwm.org.uk

Shire Publications is supporting the Woodland Trust, the UK's leading woodland conservation charity, by funding the dedication of trees.

FREEDOM IS IN PERIL

'COUGHS AND SNEEZES SPREAD DISEASES', 'Dig for victory', 'Careless talk costs lives': posters carrying slogans such as these are evocative reminders of how the Second World War was fought on the Home Front as well as the battlefield. They are now seen as classics, symbolising the way that the whole nation pulled together to defeat the enemy and build a better world, while never losing its sense of humour.

The Second World War was the first 'total war', in which the whole nation was mobilised. As a result, posters covered not only the traditional wartime themes of recruitment and war savings; they also told people to use less coal, save bones, eat more potatoes, walk more, talk less, mind the blackout, beware venereal disease, mend clothes, evacuate children, and much more besides, as the government sought to ensure that every person did his or her bit. Many thousands of posters were issued by the government, as well as by many other institutions, during these years, and some of them have become defining images of the times.

It is easy to imagine that these splendid posters were produced by a well-oiled publicity machine and were as much loved at the time as they are today. However, the real story behind how they came to be designed and produced is much more complicated, and includes spectacular failures as well as successes, while also forcing us to realise that the posters were by no means as popular during the war as they have since become.

Part of the problem was that the British public was hostile to the very idea of propaganda in the years leading up to the war. Not only was the concept associated with the Nazi state, and thus seen as the antithesis of British values, but memories of the First World War were still strong. The public had felt that recruitment propaganda then had sent young men to their deaths with a sentimental and idealised image of warfare that bore no resemblance to the reality of the trenches, and the resulting backlash was still being felt in the 1930s.

The government knew that propaganda would be unavoidable in any coming war. They were aware not only that posters had played a key part in

Opposite:
This slogan was intended for more remote areas where the danger from bombing was less immediate.
(IWM PST 14791)

Above: Like many wartime slogans, 'Dig for victory' appeared on a range of different posters. This version is by Irene Mitchell. (IWM PST 17009)

Above right: This is the best-known of cartoonist H. M. Bateman's many wartime designs.

mobilisation and morale during the previous war, but moreover that Britain was facing a Nazi enemy with a formidable publicity machine in the form of Goebbels's Ministry of Propaganda. So, while plans for the Ministry of Information (MoI) were being laid as early as 1935, the work took place under conditions of complete secrecy, for fear of a public outcry.

Well before war was declared or the Ministry even officially existed, the first posters were being designed. In April 1939 it was decided to commission an entire series of posters, which were intended to raise morale when war was declared. Despite a warning from their publicity advisors that events might overtake them, the final designs were sent to the printers in late August and so, when war was declared on 3 September, the government was able to festoon the country with posters on billboards, bus shelters and telephone boxes, in libraries and pubs, declaring, in plain text against a red background, that 'Your courage, your cheerfulness, your resolution will bring us victory'. A second poster, 'Freedom is in peril', was distributed in smaller numbers.

The campaign was prompt, but unfortunately also a resounding failure. Over 800,000 posters were produced in almost every size from billboard to telephone box, but many people claimed not to have seen them – although a few did comment that the splashes of red everywhere were at least cheering. More worryingly for the MoI, the message was seen as patronising and, worse, divisive. The image of ordinary men being sacrificed for the sake of the politicians and generals was still fresh from the First World War, and this poster, with its distinction between *your* sacrifices and *our* victory, was too much of a reminder of this.

The failure of this campaign is generally blamed on upper-class civil servants who were unable to understand the mood of the people at the start of the war; it being further suggested that the war was a democratising force that took power away from such out-of-touch individuals. There is some truth in this. The year before, a committee had concluded that domestic propaganda should come from the top down. One meeting before war was declared concluded that 'We must in short start in a Rolls Royce way, not a Ford way'. The real problem with the posters, however, was that the war had not begun as anyone had expected.

All government planning assumed that hostilities would commence with wave after wave of bombing, which would not only destroy buildings but send the public into mass hysteria and panic. Initial estimates were that for every physical death or casualty there would be at least three nervous breakdowns, resulting in as many as four million cases in the first six months.

Many people were confused by this poster because they associated resolutions with the New Year rather than war. (IWM PST 14792)

But the bombers did not come yet (and, as it turned out, when they did eventually arrive, nor did the neurosis; psychiatric admissions actually decreased during bombing raids). So the government's posters, designed to soothe the shattered nerves of a scared people, ended up looking rather silly. *The Times* commented:

> the implication that the public morale needs this kind of support, or, if it did, that this is the kind of support it would need, is calculated to provide a response which is neither academic or pious.

Home Front posters had not got off to a good start, and things did not get much better for a while. The next campaigns, while not actually annoying the public, were certainly not received with enthusiasm. The Ministry of Information did not at this point have the common touch it needed. The two officials in charge of Home Front publicity were the art historian Kenneth Clark and Harold Nicolson, a career politician

THE THREE SALVAGEERS.

The earliest posters were often neither graphically striking nor easy to understand. (IWM PST 14667)

and the husband of the writer Vita Sackville-West. They oversaw campaigns such as 'The Three Salvageers', which assumed not only a level of literary knowledge, but also a habit of allusive reading that might have come naturally to those with a university education, but not to the majority of the British population. As a result most people missed the references to Dumas and so did not much like the posters. It is probably no coincidence that the only poster of the time that was well received was 'Go to it', which used a slogan coined by the Labour minister Herbert Morrison and was designed by a professional advertising agency.

The lack of success was due not just to patrician staffing, but also to the poor management of the Ministry. Three ministers – Lord MacMillan, Lord Reith and Duff Cooper – tried and failed to get to grips with the MoI in the first years of the war, but it was repeatedly criticised for being overstaffed and too bureaucratic. Without a minister who could give it a sense of direction, it was still failing to find the common touch. In June 1940 the government was becoming increasingly worried about the levels of rumour in the country, in particular the tales initiated by Lord Haw-Haw, so they asked the Ministry to produce an anti-gossip campaign. The resulting posters and press advertisements on the theme of the Silent Column were another embarrassing failure. The campaign itself, featuring Mrs Glumpot, Miss Leaky Mouth and Mr Knowall, was not inspired, but it was supported with a wave of prosecutions for 'defeatist' talk. The public felt that not only sensible criticism but also the British sense of humour had suddenly become treasonable. For a nation of grumblers it was a step too far and Harold Nicolson wrote in his diaries that 'There is no doubt that our anti-rumour campaign has been a ghastly failure. Altogether the M of I is in disgrace again.'

This failure was perhaps more surprising because just a few months before, in February 1940, the Ministry had produced its first highly successful campaign on a very similar theme. This was 'Careless talk costs lives', designed by the *Punch* cartoonist Fougasse. After the criticisms of the 'Your courage' campaign for wastefulness, the government had learnt some lessons, so these posters were smaller, and distributed only to voluntary sites such as factories, pubs, barber shops and snack bars. Fougasse had also offered his services to the government without payment. Because of their combination of humour with a message that people wanted to believe in, they were far more popular than any other poster so far; the MoI distributed two and half million of them this way.

This one considerable triumph could not disguise the fact that the Ministry was still searching for a sense of purpose and a means of connecting with the general public. In June 1940, the 'Mightier yet' campaign was intended as reassurance for the British public facing its darkest hour after Dunkirk. But not even the Ministry itself was convinced by it: 'For want of something better we will have to plug (1) The Navy, (2) the Empire's strength, and (3) what a hell of a fine race to build up both.' Unsurprisingly, the public could not believe in the message either, and the posters fell flat.

It was only when a new Minister, Brendan Bracken, took over in July 1941 that the Ministry began to find its stride. Not only had Bracken been a newspaper editor but also, usefully, he was a protégé of Churchill. But Bracken's success was not due to his connections alone. From the start, he decided that the MoI was not there to lift the nation's morale, but simply to provide explanation and education. As he explained to the Cabinet, 'We must stop appealing to the public or lecturing at it. One makes it furious, the other resentful.' From now on, government publicity would concentrate on information, and information alone.

The Ministry of Information's first success; the slogan came from Herbert Morrison. (IWM PST 14846)

MIGHTIER YET !

Britain's Mechanised Army grows stronger every day

Opposite: Fougasse's series of 'Careless talk' posters was immediately successful, with both critics and the public.

Left: This slogan comes from 'Land of Hope and Glory', but the reference was lost on most people. (IWM PST 16861)

Bracken was right, but he was also speaking to a very different public. By the summer of 1941 the British were defending their country without any allies, and in such a state of emergency people were prepared to do whatever it took to win the war, even if this meant following a seemingly endless stream of orders from the government. This is the period that produced the Home Front slogans and posters that are best remembered today.

THE MINISTRY SAYS

ONCE THE MINISTRY OF INFORMATION had found its direction under Bracken, it went on to produce countless posters on an impossibly wide range of subjects. There was almost no part of daily life that the state did not have an opinion on during the Second World War, from what people ate to how they travelled, how they protected themselves against bombs and blackout, what they did or did not do at work, what they spent, and even whom they slept with. The stream of instructions was incessant, and one sardonic copywriter of the period saw it as almost entirely negative:

> Summed up rather arbitrarily, wartime advertising consisted largely of a long series of Don'ts:
> Don't eat too much
> Don't spend money
> Don't throw anything away
> Don't bath too often or in too much water
> Don't talk
> Don't sneeze
> Don't copulate.

He could have added 'Don't use coal or travel', as well as a couple of more positive messages, such as 'Join the armed forces' and 'Appreciate the Empire' to that list, but what characterised the posters was that they were all informational. The Ministry had now given up trying to influence that unmeasurable commodity, 'morale', and instead set out to instruct the British people on every bit of behaviour or occupation that might contribute to winning the war.

Because of the urgency of wartime and a lack of any complete records, it will probably never be possible to say exactly how many Home Front posters were produced in these years. Statistics show that the Ministry of Information worked on only a relatively small number of campaigns: for example, in 1940 it undertook just sixteen campaigns for eleven government departments.

Opposite: Wasting food was just one of the many things people were urged not to do on the Home Front.

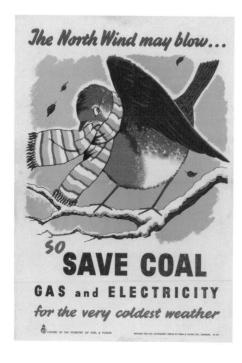

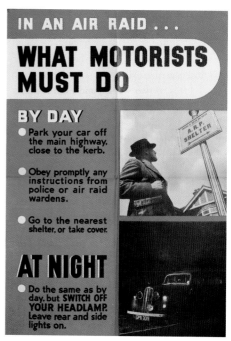

Above: Coal was rationed, but posters were used to encourage even greater economy.

Above right: Some posters carried a great deal of information and expected close attention from the viewer.

But each of these could result in a multitude of posters – there are hundreds of surviving posters on the theme of salvage alone – and these might be printed in huge numbers. By 1943 over 150,000 posters reminding people that 'Coughs and sneezes spread diseases' had been issued, and this campaign continued until the late 1940s, so many more must have been produced altogether.

In theory, all this instruction came from one source, the Home Publicity Department of the Ministry of Information. Other ministries would present the case for a campaign, which the MoI would evaluate to ensure that they thought it was achievable and would not conflict with other messages being put out. If approved, the job would either be sent out to an advertising agency or be produced in the Ministry's own General Production Department.

While that was the plan, in practice the system was a much more British kind of fudge. The two biggest-spending departments – the Ministry of Food and the National Savings Committees – refused to give up their independence and produced their own advertising throughout the war. The level of co-ordination that the Ministry aspired to was not always achieved in practice, either. A concerted campaign against August Bank Holiday travel in 1942, for example, was rather undermined by the railway companies laying on extra trains for the weekend.

But the Ministry still did an extraordinary job, producing huge quantities of posters very fast. Before the war, a poster might have taken three months to move from commission to publication; the Ministry of Information reduced this to two weeks, and even less in a few cases. In part, this was achieved by simplicity. A high-class advertising poster in 1938 would have used a subtle design with a number of coloured inks, and working out the overprinting to create the desired effects would have taken a skilled printer several weeks. To speed this up, wartime posters used a very limited number of colours (the palette was also limited due to a shortage of some inks, particularly green and yellow), most often in simple blocks that could be easily separated for printing. The result in many cases was a kind of accidental modernism, as poster designers were forced to simplify their style in order to get their message across.

One message from the railways that did not get through effectively.

Another result of austerity was smaller size, with few posters being produced any bigger than Double Crown size (30 by 20 inches), and predominantly intended for display in shops, factories and other voluntary

Trafalgar Square was one of the Ministry of Information's 'special poster sites', here displaying National Savings messages. (IWM D 5598)

15

sites, rather than on billboards. While this was mostly because of the shortage of paper (which led to some posters also being printed on both sides as an economy measure), it was also a response to the reaction to the first campaign of the war, which had, amongst many and various complaints, been criticised for its extravagance. Even so, people still complained about the waste of paper involved in government advertising, at a time when books were limited and newspapers rationed to just four or eight pages a day. A small number of larger posters was produced and a few sites, particularly in London, were used as showpiece displays for important campaigns, for example on hoardings erected around Marble Arch and Nelson's Column. People complained about this too.

Posters have often been described as essentially urban, and this was no different during the war. A town or city dweller would have been bombarded with far more instructions than someone living in a rural village, although the latter might still have come across them in the post office, school or even Women's Institute. Government guidelines, designed to prevent yet more criticisms of the waste, specified that they should be posted only 'at points where there is a considerable amount of pedestrian traffic or large bodies gathered together'. But a national distribution process led, inevitably, to some posters missing their mark. One campaign urging people to save water was not well received by those living near a large and inexhaustible Scottish loch.

Among such large numbers and wide range of subjects it is almost impossible to generalise about wartime posters. A poster could be found to prove or disprove almost any proposition; they were modern or traditional, representational or abstract, humorous or preachy. Some were very well designed, and some were considered, even at the time, not to be very good. Different posters might also have very different aims. Some, such as those identifying the types of enemy aircraft or explaining what to do in an air raid, were purely informational and therefore detailed; some, such as those telling people what to wear and how to stay safe in the blackout, were instructional and thus wanted to get a specific reaction from the viewer, while others, whether asking people to grow more vegetables or put more effort in at work, wanted to achieve a much more general result.

Many posters were entirely practical; this was for use in the aftermath of an air raid.

There are nonetheless a few common themes running through the posters. With their focus now on information, Home Front posters no longer tried to boost 'national morale' in general or abstract terms, and were much improved as a result. But some other subjects were also missing. For example, there was an almost complete lack of any images of fighting. Even at the height of the Battle of Britain, the pilots were pictured away from their aircraft, with only a single trail suggesting the fighting in which they were taking part. Militarism was seen as such an essential part of the Nazi ideology, and even a characteristic of the German race, that Britain simply could not depict itself in those terms. There were a very few exceptions to this – most notably in National Savings posters that were not produced by the MoI – but generally the act of battle was rarely shown, for fear of glorifying it. One particular example of this is the whole series of 'Careless talk' posters. There were regular calls, both inside and outside the Ministry, for images showing the direct effect of indiscretions in terms of the death of a soldier or the sinking of a ship, but such images were never produced for the general public.

Another distinctive feature of the British Home Front posters is their focus on the individual. Again, this is very much a case of the nation defining itself in contrast to the Nazi enemy, whose people were seen as subjugated to the state as a whole, with individual free will replaced by mass thought. Thus there are almost no images of serried ranks of fighting men, even from the darkest days of the war when the notion of strength in numbers might have been reassuring. On the rare occasions where more than one or two are shown together, as in the poster of the RAF pilots, each is a clearly distinguishable individual; and, of course, the title is 'The Few'.

This stress on the individual applies not just to the military subjects, but pervades almost all Home Front propaganda. In nearly every poster, there is only one person (or animal, or object even) doing his, her or its bit. To some degree, this is the result of advertising psychology, making the viewer of the poster feel that his sole effort would be important to the war. But the implicit contrast with German standardisation is still there – for example in Fougasse's 'Careless talk' posters, where the Hitlers are multiplied endlessly and repeatedly in the wallpaper.

Generalising about the styles of the posters is almost as difficult as identifying their underlying

Fougasse's ranks of identical Hitlers stand in contrast to British individualism.

"........ but for Heaven's sake don't say I told you!"

CARELESS TALK
COSTS LIVES

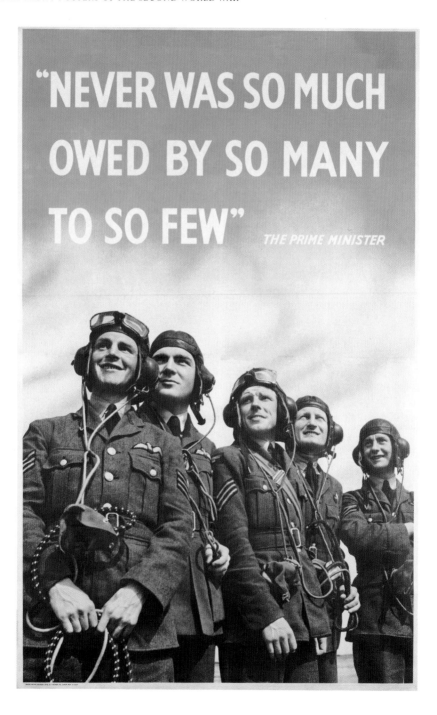

themes. At the time there was a sense that, while not every poster was or should be a work of art, the British public was being introduced to modern design by the government. While this does not entirely fit with the evidence – which is of a vast range of styles and approaches being used in the course of the war – there were some strongly modernist posters designed during and after the conflict.

In part this was a result of the circumstances of the war itself. Nazi persecution had driven many designers to Britain during the late 1930s. As foreign nationals, they were unable to serve in the forces, and so, when British designers were conscripted at the start of the war, the refugees stepped in to fill the gap as their contribution to the war effort. With their training in European modernism, designers such as Lewitt-Him, Beverley Pick, Manfred Reiss and Hans Schleger brought a new, sparer style to the posters they designed. But there were plenty of other posters that used traditional or realistic imagery to get their point across.

THE EFFECTS OF OVER-COOKING AND KEEPING HOT
Vitamin value, goodness, taste
'go up in smoke'—result is waste

Lewitt-Him's design style, although modern, suited the British love of whimsy, and the partnership's designs were very popular.

This mishmash of styles and messages was a necessary result of total war. Unlike a peacetime advertiser, who would want to reach only a particular section of the population, the government needed to speak to the entire nation, and so had to vary its tone, style and approach to make sure that everyone heard the message.

Furthermore, the posters were never designed to be seen alone but were almost always part of a wider campaign that might include leaflets, press advertising, radio broadcasts, and even short films in the cinema. So, for example, a poster that told housewives to save bread by serving potatoes would be accompanied by potato recipes in the newspapers and on the daily *Kitchen Front* radio programme that followed the news on the Home Service, while recruiting posters for the Auxiliary Territorial Service would be accompanied by newspaper advertisements that applied a much more subtle set of psychological pressures to the potential recruit.

Nevertheless, even at the time, people did try to generalise about British propaganda and how it worked. In general the British were very proud of their propaganda, even if they preferred not to think of it as such. Commentators were always very keen to distinguish between the German approach and what Britain did. John Gloag had travelled to Germany just

Opposite: Churchill's speeches often provided better slogans than the Ministry of Information could create itself. (IWM PST 14972)

Above: Bread and potatoes were never rationed during the war, but housewives were nonetheless encouraged to economise.

Above right: The Ministry of Food's posters were part of a huge campaign that also included leaflets and press advertisements.

after the Munich Crisis and compared the hysterical 'froth and foam' of totalitarian output with the commonsense approach of the British:

> No single piece of propaganda issued to the British Public by the Government has contained a threat. There have been suggestions, not bleak instructions, often conveyed with real human understanding.

From the modern perspective, this does seem to be a surprising comment. Many wartime posters, with their curt phrasing, can seem peremptory or even bossy to a public used to much less direct forms of advertising and with a very different attitude to authority. But this distinction between the Nazi propaganda machine and the humble British advertisement was very important to Britons' sense of themselves and what they were fighting for.

The other characteristic that was always identified as an essential feature of British propaganda was what John Gloag called 'Britain's secret weapon', the national sense of humour. He was not alone in feeling this: Fougasse, probably the best-known designer of this kind, argued that, while horror shut down the mind of the viewer, humour opened it, making it much easier for the message to get through. After the war, the designer Tom Eckersley remembered the humour of the posters as making a big contribution to morale: 'During some of the most trying times of the last war, when men were constantly under great strain it was the ability to appreciate amusing things which helped them to carry on.'

As well as cheering a nation under fire, humour had another advantage too: it made the posters desirable, which was particularly useful when so many were put up voluntarily. The 'Careless talk costs lives' posters were enormously popular, to the extent that 'every shopkeeper and publican wanted them', making the campaign a success almost from the start.

Bateman adapted his enormously popular 'The man who...' cartoons of the 1930s for wartime use.

ALL IN THIS TOGETHER

ALTHOUGH THE VAST MAJORITY of Home Front posters had a common theme – that everyone must try harder and do more to win the war – they did not all come from the single source of the Ministry of Information. A whole range of other institutions also produced posters, on an almost equally wide range of themes. Although they all tend to be lumped together as 'Home Front posters', their different origins meant that their aims and approaches were not always the same as the Ministry's.

Perhaps the most notable of these are the posters addressing one very specific part of the British population – the Army. Like civilians, soldiers were instructed by posters on all the usual Home Front subjects, including careless talk and growing their own food, as well as exclusively military concerns such as care of ammunition. But their posters were very different in that they had a consistent modern style; this happened because they were almost entirely produced by one remarkable man, Abram Games. Despite being only a private in the Army, by the summer of 1941, Games had his own job and department, with almost complete autonomy in how he worked. Given such freedom, he produced some of the most innovative and famous posters of the war.

Because they often cover the same themes, Games's designs tend to be included in general surveys of Home Front posters. The majority, though, would have been displayed only to serving soldiers, both at home and abroad, in barracks and messes, although those encouraging recruitment were presumably seen more widely. As a result, they are a separate case, and in particular they sometimes portray a subtly different message from the posters produced by the Ministry, as we shall see.

By 1942 Games was no longer working alone and had the services of the well-known designer Frank Newbould as his assistant, a relationship that must have had an interesting dynamic because Games was only twenty-seven and the very experienced Newbould was fifty-nine. From a design perspective, the partnership worked well, because their contrasting styles enabled them to produce posters that spoke to the men in very different ways.

Opposite: National Savings posters were almost unique in using the imagery of warfare.
(IWM PST 15596)

23

Perhaps the best-known examples of these are the set, produced for the Army Bureau of Current Affairs, with the slogan 'Your Britain, fight for it now'. Newbould's designs depict a very traditional, rural image of Britain, in which 'The White Cliffs of Dover' can almost be heard playing in the background. Games's posters, meanwhile, look forward, presenting a post-war Britain in which modern social architecture is improving the living conditions of the masses.

This was a controversial idea, and Games's poster depicting Finsbury Health Centre was never displayed because Churchill objected to the portrayal of a child with rickets as 'exaggerated and distorted propaganda'. The whole campaign was treading on dangerous ground by not only suggesting why the war was being fought, but also considering what Britain might be like when it had ended. Throughout the war, the Ministry of Information repeatedly asked for permission to run campaigns along these lines, knowing that people all over Britain were discussing this and needed to know what they were fighting for. But permission never came,

The army posters that Abram Games designed were dramatically modern in their style.

Games's work dealt with specifically military subjects as well as the more usual Home Front themes.

Frank Newbould's picture of Britain is a resolutely traditional and rural vision. (IWM PST 14887)

and so it was only the Army, where Abram Games had the freedom to design his own campaigns without interference, who ever saw these ideas in poster form. The Army posters were both more modern and more forward-looking than their civilian equivalents, and their inclusion under the general term 'Home Front' can rather distort our perceptions of both the Ministry of Information and of the Home Front itself.

Even for civilians, though, there were other sources of posters than just the Ministry of Information and some of these had as much of a

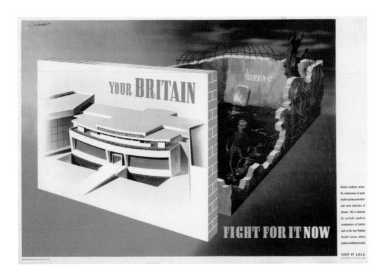

In contrast, Abram Games imagined a modern Britain after the war in order to inspire the troops. (IWM PST 2911)

Left: Some London Underground posters were addressed to staff rather than the travelling public, like this James Fitton design.

Right: Walter Spradbery's popular series of posters showed a London that was battered but defiant.

commitment to modern design and reforming ideals as the Army posters. Those who would have seen the most of this were Londoners, for the London Passenger Transport Board (LPTB) threw itself wholeheartedly into the war effort. All advertising for leisure travel was abandoned at the start of the war, and advertising spaces on both the Underground and buses were reserved solely for government publicity. But this still left room for the LPTB to print its own posters too. Many of these were instructional, helping commuters to get accustomed to the new wartime conditions of stepping out of a lit tube station into blackout, or finding your way on trains whose windows had been taped up against blast. In other cases existing campaigns, such as those persuading housewives and other non-commuters to travel between 10 a.m. and 4 p.m., took on a new urgency during the war.

As with the Ministry of Information's efforts, not every campaign was a success. 'Billy Brown of London Town', who gave travellers slightly disdainful advice in verse on how to cope with the new situations, was never much loved, the posters mainly being remembered for the sardonic extra couplets sometimes unofficially added by members of the public. But the LPTB took the hint and, just as had happened with the MoI's secrecy campaign the year before, they turned to Fougasse to make the instructions more acceptable, using humour to take the edge off the commands.

Other posters covered similar ground to the Ministry's efforts, reminding commuters to save their bus tickets for salvage, or encouraging the LPTB's own employees to greater effort in their essential war work. But, as with Games's designs for the Army, the LPTB had greater freedom than the MoI and so was able to produce more general, even inspirational, posters as well. Perhaps the most famous of these are the 'London the proud city' series by Walter Spradbery. They were very popular, not only with the travelling public, but also with the Ministry of Information, for which they solved a problem by being the kind of morale-boosting posters that it had not been permitted to commission for itself. The MoI was appreciative enough to have had the text translated into a range of languages, including Farsi and Portuguese, going on to distribute over 27,000 copies to Britain's allies.

People outside London would also have seen more than just the Ministry's own posters. Some people – although fewer as the war went on – would have come across those produced by the railways. In the first months of 'phoney war', railway advertising continued largely unchanged, and in the spring of 1940 the usual range of holiday posters, jointly produced by the resorts and the railways, was commissioned as though it was business as normal. But by May 1940 the situation was very different and leisure travel was scrapped in favour of 'Is your journey really necessary?'. This theme predominated for the rest of the war, although the Railway Executive Committee, like the LPTB, also produced a number of posters reminding their workers and the public just how essential the railways were to the war effort.

A greater number of people would have seen the publicity produced by the General Post Office (GPO). Its posters too changed from being commercial advertising to promoting the war effort. But the GPO found itself with a more intensive version of the problem facing the railways, which was that the communications it controlled – telephones, telegrams and the mail – were essential for military and planning needs. So it ended up

The office says that BILLY BROWN
Is far the nicest boss in town.
For instance, since the Blitz began,
He's organised a simple plan
Whereby his staff or most of them
Are off for home by 4.0 p.m.
We wish that every boss in town
Could do the same as BILLY BROWN

Billy Brown's good examples featured in press advertisements as well as posters.

IS YOUR JOURNEY REALLY NECESSARY?

RAILWAY EXECUTIVE COMMITTEE

Bert Thomas designed posters during the First World War, as well as illustrating this famous slogan in the Second. (IWM PST 0144)

advertising predominantly in order to tell people to use their services less, or not at all. The GPO seemed to produce more of this advertising than any other institution. Another recurring theme, caused by the need for wartime efficiency, was the need to post early, both for Christmas and for everyday mail.

Some GPO posters also advertised the Post Office Savings Bank and so overlapped with the biggest additional advertiser of all, National Savings. In theory, the National Savings Committees (one each for the four home nations) were run entirely by volunteers, separate from the government. But in practice the savings movement was so essential to the war effort that the volunteers were supported by over a thousand civil servants, and National Savings took up more of the advertising budget than any other part of the government. In 1941 it spent £834,100 on press and poster advertising; the only other department to come close to that figure was the Ministry of Food, whose total was £565,000. By contrast, the War Office spent just £48,000 producing and distributing Abram Games's Army posters.

Post your letters before noon
FOR FIRST DELIVERY NEXT MORNING
IN ENGLAND AND WALES

Early posting was one of the GPO's key messages during the war (Lewitt-Him, 1941).

For the duration of the war, the National Savings Committees had the brains behind the Mr Therm (gas) and J. Lyons (food and restaurants) advertising campaigns to advise them and employed six different agencies, but, despite these efforts, their posters are generally some of the least sophisticated and enduring in their field. They are also notably different in that, unlike almost every other poster of the time, they often used the imagery of war: detailed depictions of guns, soldiers and conflict were all used to make their case. Mass Observation, a social research organisation, put this down to the fact that savings advertising, unlike any other kind, needed to be depressing to achieve the result it required.

Left: This joint poster for the GPO and the railways was designed by Austin Cooper.

Right: The Squander Bug's appearance was almost more lovable than frightening. (IWM PST 15457)

But it is one of their other campaigns which is best remembered today: the Squander Bug, a small, hairy, swastika-covered creature who tried to tempt people, mostly housewives, to spend money on things they did not need, rather than save to help the war. This campaign was deliberately designed to be positive, in contrast to the seemingly endless stream of government prohibitions, which may have been one factor in its considerable success. The campaign worked so well that the Squander Bug was used in campaigns in Australia and the United States, where it was drawn by Dr Seuss.

One independent body did produce a sustained campaign of well-designed advertising, and that was the Royal Society for the Prevention

TAKE WARNING

WEAR GOGGLES
OR USE THE SCREEN

Tom Eckersley's
designs for RoSPA
were both modern
and highly
effective.
(IWM PST 14475)

of Accidents (RoSPA). Before the war, its focus had predominantly been on road-accident prevention, but after 1939 this changed to industrial safety instead. Preventing accidents was an important way of keeping wartime production levels as high as possible, and so in 1940 RoSPA became a service provider to the Ministry of Labour, effectively becoming an annex of the Ministry for the duration of the war.

Despite this, the society kept its editorial independence. All the posters were commissioned and approved by a publicity committee, which included Ashley Havinden, the innovative Creative Director of the W. S. Crawford advertising agency. Havinden assembled a panel of designers for this work; they included some of the most avant-garde poster designers working at the time, many of whom, such as Manfred Reiss and H. A. Rothholz, were refugees from the Continent.

RoSPA's main designer throughout the war was Tom Eckersley, who designed the majority of their posters despite have been enlisted into the Royal Air Force:

> I used to do them on leave. I'd get a 48 hour pass and go home with a particular problem in mind. I'd have between three weeks to a month to come up with an answer. In the evenings during my RAF time I'd turn it over in my mind. I'd work on it at home and my wife would then deliver it. I'd then be briefed again.

Eckersley received an OBE in 1948, as a recognition of his contribution to the Home Front war effort. This was partly because safety was one of the few areas where it was possible to prove that posters really had worked. At first industrial injuries had soared as a result of the huge numbers of new and inexperienced recruits who flooded into the factories, but, after RoSPA began its campaign, the level of workplace accidents fell to below its pre-war level.

With this almost total concentration on the war effort, it might be thought that commercial advertising would have been suspended for the duration of the war. This was certainly what the agencies believed would happen, and therefore many fired their staff when war was declared and moved skeleton offices out into the suburbs, but this turned out to be a little premature. The agencies could have survived on the amount of work they did for the government alone, even if they were doing it with reduced and sometimes unorthodox staffing, as one old hand remembered:

Opposite: James
Fitton was Art
Director at
Vernons, where
he designed these
posters for the
Ministry of Food.

At one agency, the creative staff consisted of an art director with a weak heart, a one-armed Marathon runner of about 50 who was also a devout nudist, and a short-sighted young man with a weak chest who had been Assistant Editor of *Health and Strength*.

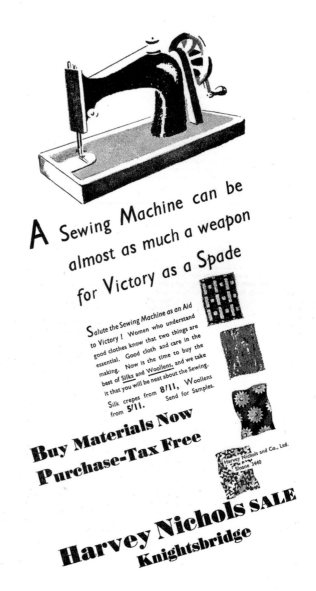

Even luxury stores such as Harvey Nichols advertised in the same tones of austerity as the government.

Later on in the war, when the importance of government advertising began to be realised, the agencies were allowed to keep staff on the grounds that they were doing a job of national importance. The relationship between the government and the advertising agencies is one that has not yet been fully explored. Many of the most famous campaigns were the work of advertising agencies commissioned by the MoI, rather than of the Ministry itself: for example, the Ministry of Food had a long-standing relationship with W. S. Crawford but also used other companies, including Mather & Crowther and Royds, while the early 'Go to it' campaign was produced by S. H. Benson. Again, the conditions of war and the lack of records make it hard to ascribe individual posters to particular agencies, but very many of the posters on display during the war, whether commissioned by the GPO or the Ministry itself, were actually the creation of advertising agencies working much as they had done before 1939.

More surprisingly, there was also plenty of commercial work for them to do as well. Companies making anything from socks to dog food followed the lead of the national institutions and harnessed their advertising to the war effort. In some cases they still had a product to sell; in others they wanted to keep their brand-name in the public eye, even though there was nothing that could be bought. But the main motivation for all of this advertising was financial. To prevent wartime profiteering, the government had decreed that any profits above the pre-war level would be taxed at 100 per cent. So, for those whose profits were going up, advertising was effectively free, because the money would otherwise have had to be handed over to the government.

Tillings, the biggest coach group before the war, commissioned and paid for these Fougasse posters.

Little of this advertising came in the form of posters, which were forbidden for any commercial purposes from 1941. But there were other ways to keep a company's name in front of the poster-reading public. The Tilling Group, the country's biggest coach group at the start of the war, donated poster spaces, possibly in their own bus stations, for a campaign about road safety, as well as buying advertisements in the newspapers for the campaign. These were the exceptions rather than the rule though, and the vast majority of posters, whether on hoardings or displayed in shops or telephone boxes, pubs or exhibitions, were exhortations directly from the government and its institutions.

DIG FOR VICTORY

BIG BROTHER IS
WATCHING YOU

FROM A MODERN PERSPECTIVE, it is difficult not to feel that these posters, with their endless stream of exhortation and instruction, even bossiness, would be hard to take for a month, let alone the five years of the war. But what did people feel about them at the time? And how much difference did they make?

These questions are relatively easy to answer in the case of a few very well-known posters. For example, the failure of the first set of posters, 'Your courage, your cheerfulness, your resolution' and 'Freedom is in peril', was well recorded when they were issued, being mentioned in Parliament as well as in numerous newspaper editorials and letters. But even in such a well-known case, it is clear that not everyone reacted in the same way. One of Mass Observation's wartime diarists, Nella Last, recorded that the poster had caused a pronounced and positive emotional reaction for her. Until that point, she had felt baffled about the war rather than patriotic, but the poster moved her very deeply, giving her a sense of her own role in the forthcoming struggle.

Successes might also be noticed at the time, as happened with Fougasse's 'Careless talk costs lives' series. This was launched to a fanfare of positive publicity, which did almost as much to get the message across as the posters themselves. But it is possible to find out much more about people's reactions, mainly because this was something that the Ministry of Information needed to know at the time. Over the course of the war, there were three ways in which they could find out: Mass Observation, the Wartime Social Survey, and Home Intelligence reports.

Initially Mass Observation got the job by default, because in 1939 it was the only organisation with any experience of testing public opinion about such matters. But the Ministry of Information had reservations about both the approach and the politics of Mass Observation, and so eventually created the Wartime Social Survey, which looked at everything from oatmeal to venereal disease, using very similar methods to Mass Observation. In addition to this, the Ministry also compiled weekly Home Intelligence reports, which combined reviews of the media with information from their regional directors to give a more impressionistic sense of popular feeling and morale.

Opposite:
'Dig for victory' appeared on a surprisingly small number of posters, but this image in particular is still well remembered. (IWM PST 0059)

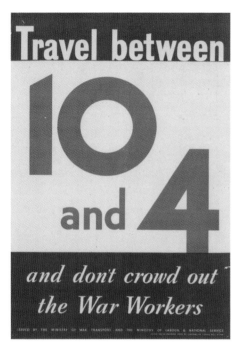

The use of all these different ways of sampling public opinion shows how far the Ministry had moved from its initial, rather imperious attitude to the public and how much it had realised that there was a gap between it and the public that needed to be closed.

Generally, it is easier to identify the posters that failed than the successes, although there are a few exceptions to this. One was the RoSPA factory safety campaigns, which clearly resulted in a much lower level of industrial accidents than would have been expected. Another campaign that worked well was one of the most famous slogans of the war, 'Dig for victory'. The only complaints came when the posters were displayed in places where there were not enough allotments to go round. Mass Observation found that propaganda had, it seemed, done more than anything else to encourage people to grow their own vegetables, although food rationing and other shortages must have helped in making the public receptive to the message.

Not every poster made the same impact. An earlier Mass Observation survey had set out to measure the results of a safety campaign that encouraged people to wear or carry something white in the blackout, launched after a sharp rise in the number of fatal accidents at night. When Mass Observation's observers went out on to the streets, they discovered that, despite the extensive advertising, only 7 per cent of the people they met were following this advice.

A more surprising failure is another of the war's best-remembered slogans, 'Make do and mend'. This campaign was launched in the summer of 1942 but, when the MoI looked at it in a Home Intelligence report at the end of the year, they found that the housewives it was aimed at had not been impressed. Most had failed to notice it at all, but, for those who did, it was an irritation. Not only did they not have time to spare on this kind of 'elaborate mending and making do', but for most working-class housewives this was nothing new, rather something they had been doing all their lives.

Housewives were the targets of more propaganda than perhaps anyone else, because so much of the work of the Home Front, from salvage to shopping for food, was their responsibility. But, as a later Home Intelligence report revealed, they mostly learned to ignore this flood of propaganda. It concluded that 'Neither posters nor leaflets are thought "to cut much ice" and are considered by some housewives to be a waste of paper'.

They were not alone in feeling this way. Throughout the war, in Parliamentary debates, MPs questioned whether, when paper for books and newspapers was so restricted, the government should be using it to print quite so many posters. This can be seen perhaps as not only a complaint about waste, but also a way of criticising the posters themselves – the belief still persisting in many quarters that propaganda on this scale was somehow not 'British'.

MPs had other complaints too. One came from the Labour MP Edith Summerskill, who took exception to a 'Careless talk' poster in 1941, asking the then Minister, Duff Cooper,

> whether he is aware that the poster bearing the words 'Be like Dad, Keep Mum', is offensive to women, and is a source of irritation to housewives, whose work in the home if paid for at current rates would make a substantial addition to the family income; and whether he will have this poster withdrawn from the hoardings?

Her objection to the sexist assumptions behind the poster seems very modern, but at the time Mass Observation reported that the poster ran into a number of other problems, most of which, interestingly, concerned issues of class. The upper and middle classes were slightly embarrassed by puns, finding them cheap and undignified, but also failed to relate to the poster because they called their parents 'Mummy' and 'Daddy', rather than 'Mum' and 'Dad', while the working classes failed to understand either of the puns – on 'kept' women, or on 'mum' meaning silent – and so missed the point of the poster until it was explained to them.

Despite appearing in both press and posters, this campaign failed to change people's behaviour.
(IWM PST 15475)

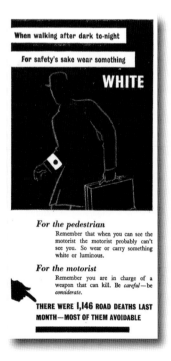

When walking after dark to-night

For safety's sake wear something

WHITE

For the pedestrian
Remember that when you can see the motorist the motorist probably can't see you. So wear or carry something white or luminous.

For the motorist
Remember you are in charge of a weapon that can kill. Be *careful* — be *considerate*.

THERE WERE 1,146 ROAD DEATHS LAST MONTH—MOST OF THEM AVOIDABLE

Above: 'Make do and mend', seen here in Donna Naschen's poster, is remembered fondly now but was not popular at the time. (IWM PST 14954)

Above right: This slogan not only enraged Edith Summerskill MP, but was widely misunderstood. (IWM PST 13916)

This complicated set of reactions reveals the wide range of interpretations that any poster had to overcome, and shows why such a diverse spread of posters was needed to reach every section of the public. Equally though, one of the biggest problems with the posters was that there were too many of them. Mass Observation recorded the situation in 1941:

Taking a short walk from the office where this report is being written, you will see forty-eight official posters as you go, on hoardings, shelters, buildings, including ones telling you:

> to eat National Wholemeal Bread
>
> not to waste food
>
> to keep your children in the country
>
> to know where your Rest Centre is
>
> how to behave in an air raid shelter
>
> to look out in the blackout
>
> to look out for poison gas
>
> to carry your gas mask always
>
> to join the AFS
>
> to fall in with the fire bomb fighters

to register for Civil Defence duties
to help build a plane
to recruit for the Air Training Corps
to Save for Victory.

Furthermore, this long list was of just one week's posters, when the war had already been going on for two years and they changed nearly every week. Mass Observation concluded that one of the biggest obstacles to effective propaganda was the sheer volume of instructions being given, often with the same level of emphasis, making it impossible for the viewer to distinguish which were the most important. People wanted to be good wartime citizens, and obedience was not the problem. They just needed to know which orders were most important to follow.

So, in the end, did these posters make any difference? Some people thought that they did. Writing at the time, *Advertisers' Weekly* unsurprisingly believed that posters made a vital contribution:

> Total War has made posters an integral part of all official instructions. Almost everybody has been affected. Thousands of appeals have to be made to the public; hundreds of directions are given… The poster can be a concise summary of, say, a half hour's speech.

One of the many and often contradictory instructions assailing the passer-by every day.
(IWM PST 13833)

But thirty years after the end of the war, Tom Harrisson, one of the founders of Mass Observation, was asked the same question and his conclusion was that they had not:

> Looked at in the short term, on the spot, in the war, neither films nor posters nor leaflets, nor any other form of deliberate propaganda directed at the Home Front, really mattered at all. The war, morale and all that was going on was at another level.

The truth is probably, as ever, somewhere between these two points of view. Perhaps the closest we can come to the experience of living among the posters is the opening chapter of the novel *1984*. The world that George Orwell is evoking draws on the state of Britain just after the war has ended. In this world the posters are everywhere, on hoardings and houses, outdoors and inside – huge, torn and flapping, oppressive, but ultimately ignored.

From the Original by ERIC FRASER

For progress in the Future—

SAVE NOW

NOW THAT THE WAR
IS OVER

THE SECOND WORLD WAR ended in August 1945, and seven months later, in March 1946, the Ministry of Information was summarily disbanded, the government believing that anything as un-British as a propaganda ministry could be justified only by war. But this was by no means the end of the Home Front poster. Hostilities might have ended, but the climate of national austerity remained for many years afterwards, and so the need for posters telling people to salvage more, use less coal, work harder and eat more cabbage was almost as great as it had ever been.

The government was still by far the biggest advertiser in the country and, just as during the war itself, the two biggest spending departments were the Ministry of Food and the National Savings Committees. Food rationing not only continued after the war (with the final restrictions not lifted until 1954) but even became more severe, with bread rationed for the first time in 1946 and potatoes in 1947, while the meat ration fell to its lowest level ever in 1951. In the case of National Savings, the end of the war also signalled a greater need for saving than ever before. With the end of the Lend-Lease agreement, Britain had to start repaying some of its massive war debts, with National Savings essential to this aim, and so a stream of posters continued to be issued – on savings, and on the virtues of green vegetables, and food economy – for many years to come.

Both of these departments still ran their own publicity campaigns, just as they had done during the war. But all other government posters and propaganda, of which there were still plenty, were now overseen by the Central Office of Information (COI). This replaced the Ministry of Information in 1946, taking over the MoI's Production Department almost in its entirety, including the two key designers, Reginald Mount and Eileen Evans, who had worked for the Ministry throughout the war.

Both as a team and on their own, Mount and Evans had designed many of the most striking wartime posters on subjects ranging from waste paper to venereal disease, and they designed many more after the war had ended. But it is almost impossible to identify which were designed after 1945 and

Opposite:
Eric Fraser's
poster for
National Savings
reflected the
desire for a better
world after the
war.

Above: The Ministry of Food was still one of the biggest advertisers in Britain well after the war had ended.

Above right: Reginald Mount and Eileen Evans often worked jointly, as with this post-war design.

which before, and this is true of almost every kind of poster produced at this time. Their concerns, from salvage to eating greens, from saving money to saving fuel, are just the same as the posters produced during the war, and very few identify whether they were commissioned by the Ministry of Information or the COI. There are a few exceptions to this. The message in 'Bones are still needed for salvage' gives a hint that this might be one, persuading people that salvage was still necessary even after the demands of the war had ended. But it is signed by its designer, Dorrit Dekk, who did not work for the COI until after she had been demobbed in 1946, and so this poster must come from the post-war period.

Similarly, some other posters can be seen displayed in the 'Britain Can Make It' exhibition of 1946, including James Fitton's 'Milk' poster and Lewitt-Him's 'Vegetabull'. Although these could have been commissioned in the last year of the war or the first year of austerity, their display in 1946, in an exhibition designed to showcase the modern, post-war world, shows how current and urgent these messages still were.

Posters were still, for the moment, a modern and impressive medium. These austerity years were the last flowering of the poster as an important way for the government to speak to the people. Newsprint continued to be rationed, and television advertising was still in the future. Furthermore, the government still had access to the network of free sites – provided by local authorities, firms and shops – that had displayed so many of the wartime propaganda posters. So, for a short while longer, the poster was dominant.

Not only were these posters produced because of the continuing austerity and national debt crisis, but the government still very much had the mentality, or at least the habit, of addressing the public on every aspect of life. When a Conservative MP wrote to *The Times* on the subject of advertising in 1948, his list of suitable subjects covers much more than the economic and financial ones that might be expected:

> Greater production and lower costs are clearly the chief national objectives.
> Others are greater exports, greater savings, greater salvage, better team
> work, better social and individual manners.

And this came from the Opposition, who were temperamentally much more opposed to this kind of propaganda than the Labour government itself. But both parties misread the national mood. When the Labour government commissioned a large campaign entitled 'We work or want' to remind people

Below left: Dorrit Dekk worked for the Central Office of Information during the late 1940s, producing several striking posters.

Below: The 'Britain Can Make It' exhibition in 1946 showed that Home Front messages were still very important even after the war.

CIVIL DEFENCE

is common sense

The Cold War produced a new set of anxieties – and a new set of posters.

of the severity of the country's situation, the public were not inspired, or even impressed. Unlike their leaders, they were by now thoroughly tired of being told what to do by posters and did not see the need for it to continue once the war had ended. It was also hard to muster much enthusiasm for the actual messages of the posters, now that the defence of the nation no longer depended on it. As one housewife commented:

I used to look upon 'making do' and renovating as a national duty and make a game of it. Now it is just a tiresome necessity.

By the mid 1950s this had all changed. Rationing was finally over, and the country was looking to live well at last. Film shorts, newspaper advertising and even the rise of television enabled the COI to direct its main efforts elsewhere and the few posters that were produced were for much less urgent subjects, such as health education and litter. The era of the Home Front poster had finally ended.

But the posters had not been forgotten. Not only were they regularly shown in exhibitions, but the designs were reprinted as postcards and tee-shirts, and reproductions were even given away with newspapers. Images such as 'Dig for victory' and 'Is your journey really necessary?' became an important part of the way in which the Second World War, and in particular the Home Front, were remembered.

Not all posters are equally remembered though. This is because their slogans and imagery have become part of the mythology of the Second World War. The years between 1939 and 1945 are imagined as an apotheosis of Britishness, where everyone did their bit, was close to the land and grew their own vegetables, threw nothing out and was simultaneously understated and heroic, but also humorous as only the British can be. The war is seen as a golden age of old-fashioned virtues, but also one where modern values, such as women working and equal shares for all, were coming into being. Thus posters are selected not necessarily for their design values or their historical significance but because they reflect this vision. Aspects of this idea are indeed true and are represented in the best-loved Home Front posters, but this myth leaves out many other aspects of the wartime experience, and so posters about rats or venereal disease tend to languish unnoticed because they are not telling people what they want to hear.

This process has been epitomised by one poster that, more than any other, has become a symbol of this British Home Front spirit, despite never having been published at the time. It is 'Keep calm and carry on'. Although it was printed in large numbers in 1939 as part of the government's first propaganda campaign, it was never used during the war and almost all the thousands of posters were pulped at the war's end. As a result it was forgotten until 2000, when a single poster turned up at the bottom of a box of second-hand books that had been bought by Barter Books in Alnwick. They hung it in their shop but received so many enquiries that they eventually reprinted a few to sell. Its popularity grew until its image could be found on everything from baby clothes to cushions, soap to golf balls. The poster is seen now not only as a distillation of a crucial moment in Britishness, but also as an inspiring message from the past to the present in a time of crisis.

But, as the first chapter has already shown, to think of 'Keep calm and carry on' in this way requires that we forget some important facts about how it came into being. That first set of propaganda posters, which also included 'Your courage, your cheerfulness, your resolution' and 'Freedom is in peril', was seen at the time not as inspiring, but as a patronising and rather insulting failure. Moreover, 'Keep calm and carry on' was created because it was assumed that in the face of sustained bombing the British public would have a collective nervous breakdown and so keeping calm and carrying on was exactly what they were not going to do. But this inconvenient history tends not to be repeated very often, because it gets in the way of the myth. People much prefer to believe that this image is an inspiring message from the past to the present, reminding us of how the British got through the Second World War with a stiff upper lip, a lot of cabbage and some posters, whereas in reality it is the record of a rather embarrassing failure of both planning and imagination.

There are so many Second World War Home Front posters, with more possibly waiting to be discovered in another box somewhere, that it is

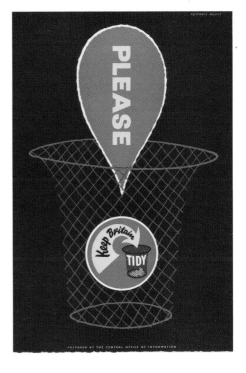

This 'Keep Britain tidy' design by Reginald Mount is typical of the less urgent messages produced in the 1950s.

PLEASE

Keep Britain TIDY

PREPARED BY THE CENTRAL OFFICE OF INFORMATION

possible to create almost any kind of story from them. But the way they tend to be used nowadays does a disservice to the posters and the people who lived through the war. To pretend that this was nothing more than an idyll in which the British were at their best, inspired and enthused by cheerful posters that encouraged them to even greater efforts, is too simple; the picture, is, as ever, much more subtle and complicated than that. Some posters were successful or well-designed, some even both, but others were failures or irritating, and even during the war the public found the constant torrent of exhortation infuriating; some just shut it out. It will probably never be possible to say exactly what these posters did or did not contribute to the war effort, and whether they reflected the real experience of the times, but the least we can do is to look at them properly, to find out the full truth of what they were, and still are, saying.

Above: This poster was reprinted by Barter Books in 2001, becoming an unexpected success.

Right: The 'Keep calm' slogan spread from posters on to almost every item imaginable.

PLACES TO VISIT

Imperial War Museum, Lambeth Road, London SE1 6HZ. Telephone: 020 7416 5320. Website: www.iwm.org.uk. The IWM holds the main collection of Home Front posters, with over twenty thousand in their collection. A selection is always on display as part of its exhibitions, but a wider range can be seen in its online archive at www.iwmcollections.org.uk.

Other online archives that contain Home Front posters include the British Postal Museum and Archive, which contains General Post Office posters (www.postalheritage.org.uk/page/collections), and the London Transport Museum collection (www.ltmcollection.org/posters/index.html).

Even the Ministry of Information realised that the public was overwhelmed by the sheer volume of official instructions.

FURTHER READING

Aulich, James. *War Posters: Weapons of Mass Communication.* Thames & Hudson, 2011.

Bownes, David, and others. *London Transport Posters: A Century of Art and Design.* Lund Humphries, 2008. Includes chapter on wartime posters.

Lewis, Bex. *The Planning, Design and Reception of British Home Front Posters of the Second World War.* Unpublished PhD thesis: along with more of Dr Lewis's research, it can be found on her website, www.ww2poster.co.uk.

Moriarty, Catherine; Rose, June; and Games, Naomi. *Abram Games, Graphic Designer: Maximum Meaning, Minimum Means.* Lund Humphries, 2003. Includes section on Games's war work.

Rennie, Paul. *Modern British Posters: Art, Design and Communication.* Black Dog Publishing, 2010. More general overview but includes much wartime material.

Slocombe, Richard. *British Posters of the Second World War.* Imperial War Museum, 2010. Good illustrated survey.

What do I do...

with these "What do I do" announcements?

I read them carefully wherever I see them, because they contain *official* information in a short form on the subjects they deal with.

I cut them out and keep them, because today's subject may be an answer for tomorrow's problem.

I see to it that my family read them too. "I never knew" is no excuse today!

Cut this out—and keep it!

Issued by the Ministry of Information
Space presented to the Nation
by the Brewers' Society

INDEX